THE NATIONAL TRUST

Coleton Fishacre

Kingswear, Devon

ALAN POWERS

Coleton Fishacre

A Garden by the Sea

Step into the Hall, turn to the left, and there is the Flower Room. Turn to the right, and you face a dial showing High Water in Pudcombe Cove. Here at once are the two reasons for Coleton Fishacre – the garden and the sea.

Coleton Fishacre was built in 1923–6 for Rupert D'Oyly Carte, whose father Richard had been the impresario behind the operettas of Gilbert and Sullivan. Rupert developed the business empire he inherited, which included the Savoy Hotel and Claridge's in London. In the changed conditions after the First World War he successfully gave his patrons what they wanted in the theatre, restaurants or hotel suites. The interiors at Coleton Fishacre evoke the modernity of the Jazz Age, while their architectural casing is perfectly dressed for a weekend in the country. Yet there is no apparent conflict.

Apart from the built-in decorative features which have always remained in the house, such as the pictorial map in the Library, the decorative bathroom tiles and dining-room light-fittings, only a few items of furniture were kept when Rupert D'Oyly Carte's daughter Bridget sold Coleton Fishacre in 1949. The rooms had in any case been sparsely furnished in the taste of their time, partly because it was a house where the emphasis was on outdoor activities – sailing, swimming and tennis, fishing, riding and gardening.

Oswald Milne (1881–1967), the architect of Coleton Fishacre, was an assistant to Sir Edwin Lutyens from 1902 to 1905, when he set up his own practice. Milne was less inventive than Lutyens, the architect of Castle Drogo and New Delhi, but in his best works he showed his debt to the Arts and Crafts architects inspired by William Morris and Philip Webb. They believed in the positive power of simple design, reinforced by the highest standards of craftsmanship. Milne's work at Coleton Fishacre thus has roots going back some 50 years in the history of English architecture, although it has an unmistakable look of a house of its time.

The National Trust acquired Coleton Fishacre in 1982 as part of its Enterprise Neptune campaign, chiefly in order to link up the south Devon coastal path. The quality of the garden was immediately recognised, and this was opened to the public, while the house was let to private tenants. In 1982 Oswald Milne's design for Coleton Fishacre was still too recent to be easily evaluated, but it can now be better appreciated as his finest work and one of the most successful smaller country houses to be built in the 1920s.

Rupert D'Oyly Carte; cartoon by Autori (Peter Parker collection)

The Lalique tulip uplighters in the Dining Room are among Coleton's finest Art Deco details

(*Left*) Open-air leisure on the terrace

(*Opposite*) Sheltered to the north, Oswald Milne's design for the D'Oyly Cartes' house looks over the descending garden to the sea

The D'Oyly Carte Family

Richard D'Oyly Carte (1844–1901) came from a musical family in London and composed operas as a young man. He found his profession as a concert agent and theatrical manager in 1870. Five years later, he promoted a one-act operetta, *Trial by Jury*, with words by a barrister, W.S. Gilbert, and music by one of the most talented younger composers of the period, Arthur Sullivan.

The success of Gilbert and Sullivan's combination of good tunes, mild social satire, verbal ingenuity, absurd plot line and burlesque of theatrical convention increased with further productions. Following the 700-night run of their third major piece, *HMS Pinafore* (1878), D'Oyly Carte formed an exclusive business alliance with Gilbert and Sullivan and built the Savoy Theatre off the Strand, followed soon afterwards by the Savoy

Richard D'Oyly Carte, the impresario behind Gilbert and Sullivan; cartoon by Spy (Melvyn Tarran collection)

An early programme for *The Yeomen of the Guard*, first performed in 1888 (Peter Parker collection)

Hotel. The annual profits for the three men reached £60,000, and D'Oyly Carte often had as many as five touring companies performing Gilbert and Sullivan in Britain and the United States at the same time. Appropriately for a West Country subject, the first performance of *The Pirates of Penzance* (1879) was held at the Royal Bijou Theatre, Paignton, in Devon.

At the Savoy Theatre, the Gilbert and Sullivan premières every year or two were major social events. Seven new operas were produced during the 1880s, of which *Iolanthe* (1882), *The Mikado* (1885) and *The Yeomen of the Guard* (1888) are perhaps the best-known. Sullivan would conduct the première himself, striking up the overture, which was often written the night before the opening. The songs were sung around the piano in homes all over the world, and many of Gilbert's phrases have entered the English language.

A financial quarrel between Gilbert and D'Oyly Carte in 1891, during the run of *The Gondoliers*, was eventually patched up, and two further operas written, but these failed to enter the permanent repertory of the D'Oyly Carte Opera Company.

The success of the operas was due to their acceptability to the middle classes as well as to Queen Victoria; earlier, musical theatre was considered morally offensive. D'Oyly Carte also ran his opera companies with propriety and helped to make the stage a career open to talented and respectable singers. His attempts to promote grand opera, which involved the construction of the Palace Theatre at Cambridge Circus, were less successful, but he left a flourishing business at his death in 1901.

Richard D'Oyly Carte had two children by his first marriage to Blanche Prowse: Lucas (b.1872) a barrister who died of tuberculosis in 1907, and Rupert (1876–1948), who is said to have been the inspiration for P.G. Woodhouse's character Psmith. The latter succeeded his stepmother Helen Couper-Black as manager of the family businesses.

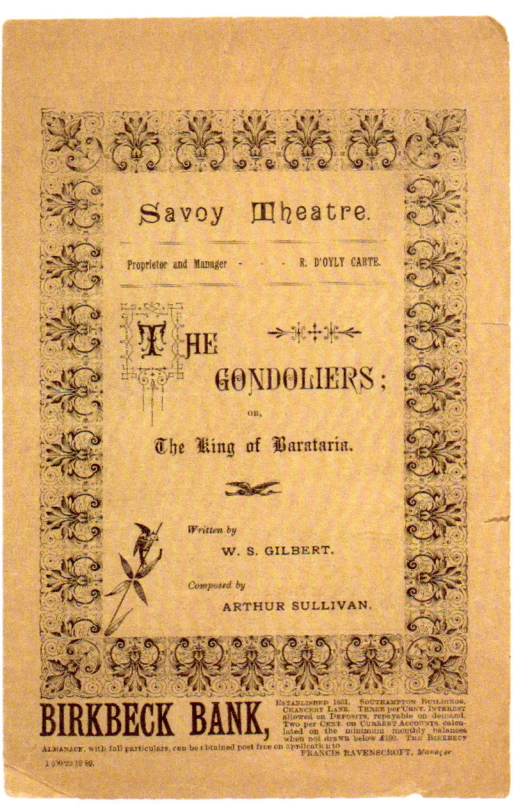

The Gondoliers (1889) was the climax of Gilbert and Sullivan's decade of success at the Savoy Theatre (Peter Parker collection)

Modern Houses in Devon

Modern architecture in Devon began with the building of Castle Drogo, designed by Sir Edwin Lutyens in 1910. Because it was conceived as a castle, it is abstract in form, and externally the granite is cut with hardly any decoration or mouldings. Its grandeur is achieved as much by the illusion of scale as by sheer size, unlike some of the late Victorian country houses. After the First World War, building a country house was a more expensive business, and house plans were simplified to suit less formal lifestyles and fewer servants. Only a few houses in Devon were built by the traditional landowning class, such as Ashcombe Tower near Dawlish, which was constructed in 1934 for the MP for Totnes, Ralph Rayner, who also farmed the estate. Designed by a young architect, Brian O'Rorke, Ashcombe Tower is conservative in style on the outside, but more modern inside, with a high standard of comfort and many specially made pieces of furniture and textiles.

The majority of new houses were holiday or weekend homes by the coast like Coleton Fishacre. In the 1920s, the architect Oliver Hill designed a picturesque fairy-tale cottage almost on the beach at Croyde, near Ilfracombe, for two women playwrights. Matthew Dawson designed a romantically sited mansion for Archibald Nettlefold on Burgh Island in 1929, where he planned to entertain his theatrical friends, which later became a hotel.

The most extensive place of architectural patronage in Devon between the wars was Dartington Hall, where Leonard and Dorothy Elmhirst took over a ruined medieval mansion and a run-down estate in 1925 in order to start an experiment in rural regeneration and progressive education. Oswald Milne worked for them on a number of projects, including staff houses, college buildings and a textile mill, before he was displaced by the Swiss-born New York architect William Lescaze. In 1930 Lescaze argued that Milne's polite English Georgian and vernacular no longer served modern needs or took advantage of modern inventions and techniques. The Elmhirsts agreed to Lescaze designing High Cross House on the Dartington estate for the new Headmaster, W.B. Curry. Completed in 1932, it was one of the earliest Modern Movement houses in England, with smooth white walls (and a wing painted blue), large metal-framed windows and roof terraces. High Cross, which has recently been restored and opened to the public by the Dartington Hall Trust, led to other commissions for Lescaze at Dartington, although the attempt to market his houses at Churston Bay in 1936–7 was a failure.

A dramatic corridor at Castle Drogo by Sir Edwin Lutyens, whose work influenced Oswald Milne at Coleton Fishacre

The towering south-east corner of Castle Drogo; watercolour by Cyril Farey

(*Opposite*) High Cross House, the Modern Movement house built for the Headmaster of Dartington School in 1932

The living room of Ashcombe Tower is decorated with Marion Dorn carpets

The house under construction in 1925

The Building of Coleton Fishacre

Rupert D'Oyly Carte and his wife, Lady Dorothy, found the site for their house from the sea, while sailing their yacht between Brixham and Dartmouth. They rented a house in nearby Kingswear so that they could oversee construction. The roadwork was begun in January 1925, and the house was completed in June 1926. The stone was quarried by blasting rock in the lower part of the combe, which was transported to the site by a small temporary railway. The contractors were E.H. Burgess of Berners St, London.

A 'motor house' on the drive, housing the D'Oyly Cartes' Bentley, as well as a chauffeur's flat and two staff cottages, was less expensively built out of brick with a rendered finish.

The radiating granite paving in the forecourt, set on a slope, is a striking feature among many touches of fine craftsmanship in the house, whose quality is to be found in the integrity of its materials and the sensitive and lively effect created by small irregularities of stone colour, surface and shape within the overall plainness, both of walls and roofs. The quality of stone-walling extends from the house to the garden, including the roofed loggia, from which the sea was clearly visible before the trees grew to their present size (see illustration on pp.20–21) The Gazebo above the quarry still provides such views. On the beach at Pudcombe Cove, the D'Oyly Cartes built a bathing hut and a tidal bathing pool in concrete, both of which still partly remain.

Coleton and the Idea of Modern

The 1920s was a period in British architecture which even experts have difficulty navigating. The stylistic labels, like the architecture, seem to follow from the pre-1914 period. Coleton Fishacre belongs to the Arts and Crafts movement of the 1890s in its simpler forms, but avoids any exaggeration of form or rusticity. Writing in *Country Life* in 1930, Christopher Hussey wanted simply to call it 'modern', but was aware that this word 'carries implications of affectation', having already been appropriated to describe the International Style, an architecture with similar intentions of simplicity and honesty, but much more revolutionary aesthetics and construction methods. If there is a genuine link between the 1890s and the 1920s, as many historians of the time wanted to believe, it can be seen at Coleton Fishacre as readily as in more obvious precursors of Modernism, such as the houses of Charles Rennie Mackintosh.

The granite paving, laid in a radiating pattern, is a striking feature of the entrance court

(*Below*) The newly completed house from the south, showing the open character of the garden in its early years

The Exterior

The plan of Coleton Fishacre consists of three arms of a Y, of unequal length, forming an entrance courtyard to the north-east and a garden terrace to the south. The third space is the service entrance, against the slope of the hill on which the house stands. Milne did not invent this plan, but used it skilfully and kept consistent lines of roof ridges and eaves running through the house, giving it a sense of unity.

The geometry of the roofs, including the semicircular bay on the garden front and the set-back roof ridge of the service quarters with its long 'catslide' coming forward over the garden loggia, is amplified by the fine quality of the Delabole stone slates and the way they are carried around the curves. The Dartmouth shale stone for the walls, with its mixture of blues, greens and browns, gains an unconscious sense of belonging from having been quarried on the estate. It is beautifully laid with thick mortar joints. The leaded casement windows are housed in unpainted oak subframes. There is almost no decoration on the outside of the house, apart from the wrought-iron weathervane supplied by Negretti & Zambra, and the stone sundial on the garden front, which was carved by Herbert W. Palliser in the style of the pharaoh Tutankhamun, whose tomb had been discovered in 1922.

Comic fishermen in silhouette on the weathervane

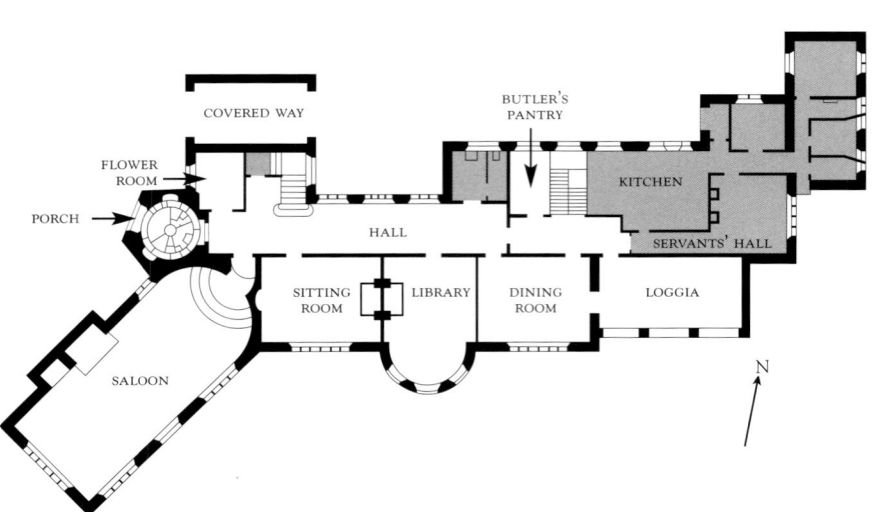

Coleton was furnished in the style Osbert Lancaster christened 'Curzon Street Baroque'

The Interior

Internally, the effects are simple but achieved with a greater smoothness of material. Milne managed to stay poised on the edge between an identifiable historical style and the kind of inevitable form that could result from following two doctrines popular in the 1920s – 'fitness for purpose' and 'truth to materials'. The choice of a continuous panelled stair baluster of limed oak avoids the need to introduce Georgian detail, while the fireplaces and doorcases use the 17th-century form of bolection moulding which dies back into the wall at its outer edge. Walls run into ceilings with a smooth continuous cove. The austerity of these forms is relieved by Art Deco details, such as the stepped door surround in the Saloon (matched by a stepped mirror over the fireplace), and the hexagonal ceiling lights with their mixture of real and fake tassels. In the bathrooms, the pictorial tiles from Carter's of Poole reveal the whimsical character of the period. The mixture of Baroque and oriental furnishings, tastefully spaced out in white rooms with accents of strong colour, was typical of the 1920s. The general style was illustrated and described by Osbert Lancaster as 'Curzon Street Baroque' in his book, *Homes Sweet Homes* (1939).

The bedroom corridor in 1930

Rupert D'Oyly Carte

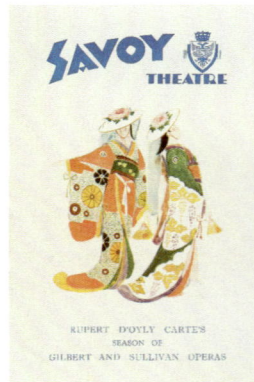

The 1926 Savoy Theatre season featured a new production of *The Mikado* with costumes designed by Charles Ricketts

Rupert D'Oyly Carte rebuilt the Savoy Theatre in 1929 with Art Deco interiors by Basil Ionides (Matthew Weinreb)

Rupert D'Oyly Carte as Patron

Rupert D'Oyly Carte succeeded his father as Chairman of the Savoy Hotel Company in 1903, and ten years later took over the management of the Opera Company from his stepmother. Little had been done since 1900 to reflect changes in style, and the wardrobe mistress was still issuing the female chorus with red flannel knickers. The First World War changed many expectations about style, although light entertainment and luxury hotels remained in demand. In modernising his dual legacy, D'Oyly Carte showed a discerning patronage of artists and designers, who, while not revolutionary, were capable of bringing a fresh and colourful approach to the reinterpretation of the past.

After 1918 fashion swung sharply against everything Victorian, but since Gilbert and Sullivan were often ridiculing Victorian conventions, their work escaped becoming dated. The art of the stage designer had advanced from the realism of the 19th century to a wittier, more poetic sense of evocation.

Rupert D'Oyly Carte commissioned new sets and costumes for *The Mikado* in 1926 from the distinguished artist Charles Ricketts, who aimed for 'beauty, humour and an element of surprise'. His costumes, accurately based on Japanese models of the period around 1720, were praised as 'almost embarrassing in their wealth. They lend themselves to every angle of the body,

sometimes graceful or funny, sometimes both.' Ricketts also redesigned the sets and costumes for *The Gondoliers*, while another artist, George Sheringham, treated both *The Pirates of Penzance* and *Patience* to great acclaim.

Rupert D'Oyly Carte introduced new interiors in a refined French Art Deco style to Claridge's and the Savoy, and in 1929 rebuilt the Savoy Theatre to designs by Frank Tugwell, with interiors by Basil Ionides, creating a shimmering, silver-leafed shrine to modern comfort and refinement. The multicoloured seating is typical of his whimsical attention to detail. He saw a bed of zinnias in Hyde Park and instructed his designer to match their red, orange and yellow shades with a random scattering of colours. A somewhat similar effect was achieved in the servants' quarters at Coleton, which originally had bright black, pink and orange marbled doors and a red tiled floor.

Oswald Milne was commissioned to build the new ballroom wing at Claridge's in 1930, and D'Oyly Carte personally tested all the baths in the showroom, sitting in them in his morning coat, top hat and spats. The ballroom entrance included bold geometric carpets by Marion Dorn, whose work was also introduced to Coleton Fishacre in the 1930s. One of Rupert's last commissions – the redesign of *The Yeomen of the Guard* by Peter Goffin in 1939 – was modernist in its austerity.

The conductor Sir Thomas Beecham was a friend of the D'Oyly Cartes; cartoon by Autori (Peter Parker collection)

Programme for the 1929-30 Gilbert and Sullivan season at the Savoy

The Ballroom at Claridge's in the new extension designed by Oswald Milne for Rupert D'Oyly Carte; photographed in 1930

Michael D'Oyly Carte

Life at Coleton Fishacre

Rupert D'Oyly Carte married Lady Dorothy Gathorne-Hardy, the younger daughter of the 2nd Earl of Cranbrook, in 1907. She had dark hair and suited the costume of Ruth, the pirate 'maid of all work' from *The Pirates of Penzance*, which she sometimes wore as fancy dress. While Dorothy lived permanently at Coleton, Rupert came down from London by train every Friday evening for the weekend. They loved the outdoor life, being very keen on fishing and shooting, and often sailing their yacht out on weekend jaunts to the south Cornwall gardens in search of inspiration. On Saturday mornings they would walk round their own garden together discussing their plans for the planting. They also enjoyed entertaining: weekend guests included musicians like the conductor Sir Malcolm Sargent and painters such as Charles Ricketts (designer of the 1926 *Mikado* costumes), who came for bridge parties and were put to work weeding the garden. The informal, but luxurious, quality of the house seems to have been a perfect match for a life of pleasure.

The D'Oyly Cartes had two children, Bridget (1908–85) and Michael, who was killed in a car accident in Switzerland in 1932. This tragedy undermined their

(*Right*) The D'Oyly Cartes in fancy dress with their company: Rupert in ruff, Lady Dorothy in Ruth's costume from *The Pirates of Penzance* (*above*), and their daughter Bridget kneeling (Peter Parker collection)

marriage, and they separated in 1936. In 1939 Brig. Gen. E.H. and Kitty Llewellyn moved into the house after their own nearby home had been taken over by an evacuated school. Kitty ran the household and oversaw redecoration, which included repainting the window frames slate blue.

After attending Dartington School as one of its earliest pupils, Bridget D'Oyly Carte married her cousin, later the 4th Earl of Cranbrook, in 1926, a marriage which lasted only four years. She did not marry again, but assisted her father, and from 1939 to 1947 was involved in child welfare work in London. Bridget (who became Dame Bridget in 1975) devoted herself after 1948 to running the opera company in succession to her father. Described by Sir Hugh Wontner as 'by nature shy and retiring, characteristics she inherited from her father', Bridget faced the cessation of copyright in the operas in 1961 with practical measures that ensured continuing performances until 1982 by a newly constituted company under her own direction. She also formed the D'Oyly Carte Opera Trust as a charitable organisation to promote future productions. She was a director of the Savoy Hotel group and exercised a strong influence on matters of design and decoration. After selling Coleton Fishacre in 1949, because it was too far from London, she bought Shrub's Wood, near Chalfont St Giles, an important example of the Modern Movement in architecture designed by Eric Mendelsohn and Serge Chermayeff in 1934–5, where she enhanced the garden with rare trees and shrubs.

Later Owners

In 1949 Coleton Fishacre was bought by Rowland Smith, a well known London motor trader and owner of the Palace Hotel in Torquay. Together with his wife, Freda, he maintained the house and garden with great care until his death in 1979. The estate was offered to the National Trust by Freda just before her own death in January 1982. The Dining Room furniture and the Marion Dorn carpets were left behind, and Bridget D'Oyly Carte took only a small number of items to her new home in Buckinghamshire. During 1997–8 the National Trust began to furnish the house ready for opening to the public for the first time in 1999. This process is ongoing and changes will occur from time to time as the current collection is refined and developed to reflect the house's heyday in the 1930s.

Bathing in Coleton's tidal swimming pool

Edward Bawden's bathroom tiles feature recreations typical of the 1920s

The conductor Sir Malcolm Sargent was a regular visitor to Coleton; cartoon by Autori (Peter Parker collection)

Tour of the House

The Porch & Hall
The polygonal porch is circular on the inside, with a curved bench made specially to fit against the walls. The *Cave Canem* warning on the doormat was in earnest, as the D'Oyly Cartes kept a boisterous dalmatian and Cairn terriers. The mat conceals a central roundel carved with Rupert and Dorothy's initials and the date the house was completed – 1926.

The Porch leads into the long, straight hall, from which the stairs mount to the left. Next to the staircase is the small Flower Room, in which cut flowers from the garden were arranged for display in the house. On the wall opposite is a clock dial used to indicate High Water in Pudcombe Cove.

Turn left up the stairs.

The Staircase
Above the stair landing, the D'Oyly Cartes hung a large painting by Walter Richard Sickert (1860–1942) of St Mark's, Venice, painted about 1896–7, which, in Christopher Hussey's words, provides a "splash of mellow colour on the whitewashed walls". This was given by Dame Bridget to the British Council as a thank you for all the amateur G & S productions it had supported around the world. Note how only the top rail of the panelled staircase balustrade is varnished.

The Bedroom Corridor
Above the stairs is another of the honeycomb ceiling lights also found in the Entrance Hall; there are simpler versions along the corridor.

Turn right into the first of the bedrooms, which is now given over to an exhibition about Coleton Fishacre and the D'Oyly Cartes. Another of the bedrooms houses an exhibition about the conservation of 20th century materials, and another has a temporary exhibition.

The Bedrooms
There are seven bedrooms on this floor of which four are furnished. As no original furniture for the upper floor survives from the D'Oyly Carte era, these have been furnished with introduced Heal's oak bedroom furniture which evokes the 1930s.

The National Trust has opened Lady Dorothy D'Oyly Carte's bedroom, as it was shown in a *Country Life* photograph of 1930 with curtains, seat-covers and cushions in a bold floral fabric designed in 1919 by the French artist Raoul Dufy, who produced some of the finest designs of the period.

The tide-indicator in the Hall

The staircase in 1930, with the Sickert hanging over the half-landing

St Mark's, Venice, by W.R. Sickert (British Council), is the most important picture in the house

(*Opposite*) Lady Dorothy's Bedroom in the 1930s, with the curtains and cushions made up in 'Les Arums' printed linen, a bold black and cream pattern designed by the French artist Raoul Dufy in 1919

(*Top and bottom*) Edward Bawden bathroom tiles

(*Right*) The Loggia in 1930, before the trees had obscured the view of the sea

The Bathrooms

The two bathrooms retain many of their original fittings, including the Doulton and Co. sunken baths with their green glass soap dishes and large blue glass sponge bowls. The tiled surrounds feature a series of pictorial tiles designed by Edward Bawden (1903–90) for Carter's of Poole, a Victorian firm which became part of the campaign for good design in the 1920s and employed Bawden soon after his graduation from the Royal College of Art, where his outstanding talents as an illustrator and designer had already been recognised. These tiles show comic scenes of outdoor life, appropriate for Coleton. Some are traditional, like the fisherman, some modern, like the open car rushing downhill.

Descend the servants' staircase.

The Servants' Quarters

The D'Oyly Cartes were wealthy enough to afford a substantial staff at Coleton: butler, housekeeper, housemaid and cook working in the house, as well as a chauffeur and six gardeners outside.

Turn right into

The Butler's Pantry

The Belfast sink with its beech draining boards are original. The large glazed cupboard is a slightly later introduction.

Cross the lobby to

The Dining Room

The Dining Room is the most recognisably

The Dining Room in 1930

'Curzon Street Baroque' room in the house, with its blue scagliola table-top evoking the sea, and matching side-tables providing rounded ends for the main table, if required. A bell push was also made to match, but from real lapis lazuli, a rare blue stone. The curved wrought-iron supports of the tables are typical of European taste from c.1912 onwards, with their repeating curves recalling the 18th century Baroque. These are positioned below decorative opalescent glass wall lights with a moulded design of tulips. The Paris cityscape, *Boulevard St Germain*, was painted in 1930 by Bassett Wilson.

In 1930 a red lacquer cigar cabinet stood between the side-tables, below a concave mirror in a Regency gilt frame, which has been restored to the room. The floor was originally carpeted with a simple grid pattern.

The Dining Room opens on to the loggia, which also had a table, where the D'Oyly Cartes and their guests would usually have had their meals in summertime.

Leave by the far door and turn into the ground floor corridor, the first door on the left leads to

The Llewellyns, who lived at Coleton during the Second World War, dining al fresco

The Library

The Library occupies the bow on the south front of the house. It is simply fitted with pine shelves and lit by simple translucent alabaster uplighters above them. The set of four Art Deco chairs is original.

The overmantel includes a wind dial (a feature found in several Lutyens houses), and the way this is inserted into the painted map below is also reminiscent of Lutyens's mannerism. The map painting is by George Spencer Hoffman (1875–1950), who trained as an architect and may have known Oswald Milne in the office of Sir Arthur Blomfield in the first years of the century. After the First World War he specialised as a watercolorist and executed a similar map, 'showing the hills, church and the houses of the Great and the Good, within some seven miles' for John Fothergill, the gentleman landlord of the Spread Eagle at Thame, a place visited by the D'Oyly Cartes. His overmantel at Coleton Fishacre appears as a realistic bird's-eye view, although the house itself and other features, such as Rupert D'Oyly Carte sitting overlooking the combe with a favourite dalmatian, are overscaled without suffering any severe discrepancy. The indented coastline makes it a particularly suitable subject for this kind of treatment.

The next door on the left leads to

The Library overmantel combines Spencer Hoffman's bird's-eye view of Coleton with a wind dial

Boy blowing on a conch shell; by J. Havard Thomas, 1893 (Sitting Room)

A moment of drama: the steps down into the Saloon in 1930

(*Right*) The ceiling light in the Sitting Room as it appeared in 1930

The Sitting Room

This small sitting room, largely used by Lady Dorothy for afternoon tea, writing and relaxing, has another handsome chimneypiece, here carved from Hoptonwood marble rich in fossils. The broad mullioned windows have black Staffordshire tile sills, like all the windows in the house. The skirting boards, here and elsewhere, were originally painted black to match. The semicircular niche was designed for displaying flowers or china, and is smooth plastered in contrast to the rougher walls.

The last room on the left is

The Saloon

A short curved passage opens out on to stage-like steps leading down into the Saloon, a generously proportioned room almost 12 metres long, which is set at an angle to the rest of the house to exploit the views down over the garden. The simple Siena marble chimneypiece was supplied by Messrs Jenkins & Son of Torquay. The plaster was deliberately left with a rough finish, which was subtly accentuated by the Art Deco alabaster wall-lights.

The floor was laid with Indian gurgen wood and in the photograph published in *Country Life* in 1930 is shown with a large French-style carpet spanning the room and a suite of upholstered furniture in chintz covers with smaller antique pieces around the walls. In the 1930s a new carpet, runner and two matching rugs by Marion Dorn were introduced, which have remained in the house ever since. Dorn (1896–1964), who came from California, was the leading freelance textile designer of the inter-war period in England, and favoured large-scale patterns for her carpets, in which the texture of the weave was as important as the simple combinations of colour.

The present furnishings include an Art Deco settee and chairs, a mirror-top coffee table of the 1930s and a Blüthner grand piano.

Low windows with a coved ceiling increase the sense of space in the Saloon, photographed in 1930

The Garden

The garden at Coleton, like several in the South West, descends from open views around the house at the head of the narrow combe, through increasingly jungle-like vegetation, following the course of the stream down to the sea at Pudcombe Cove. The terraces and the walled Rill Garden beside the house provide a formal introduction to the wilder garden below.

Rupert and Lady Dorothy D'Oyly Carte were both enthusiastic gardeners. Their first priority was to provide protection from the prevailing winds, and even before the house had been completed, they were planting shelter belts of pines, holm oak and sycamore on the bare ridges, with advice from Edward White of the landscape designers Milner & White. Rupert and Lady Dorothy were then able to give free rein to their gardening skills, experimenting with trees and shrubs from around the world. To their far-sighted talent for placing plants we owe many of the finest vistas in the garden. Lady Dorothy was particularly keen on roses and hydrangeas, Rupert on water features. Planting continued throughout the 1930s, and a variety of exotic trees and shrubs was added even during the war years.

The acidic soil, overlying Dartmouth shale, with water moving through the valley in many places, makes it suitable for the widest range of plants, including succulents from the Canary Isles and Tree Ferns from New Zealand. Thanks to the sea and the stream, atmospheric humidity is high, although rainfall averages only 925mm (36in) a year. So many moisture-loving plants grow to perfection beneath the tree canopy and due to the mild climate, you will see species growing here to an exceptional size which can survive outside in few other places in Britain.

Coleton through the Seasons

Spring starts very early at Coleton, when the bowl of the garden is filled with the colours of rhododendrons, Chilean Fire Trees, azaleas, magnolias, dogwoods and camellias, backed by the varied foliage of conifers and broad-leaved trees. In summer the hydrangeas take the stage, their billowing swags of rich and pale blue flowers echoing the tones of the summer sea. Autumn sees the changing colours of leaves and the appearance of berries on Spindle Trees, rowans and many other trees and shrubs. In winter the shapes of the bare trees are revealed against the backdrop of evergreens and set off by spire-like hollies and the varied forms of conifers.

The 'candle' of an *Echium pininana*

Lady Dorothy in her gardening clothes

Flowers of Chilean Lantern Tree (*Crinodendron hookerianum*)

Spring on Seemly Terrace with *Halium umbellatum*, *Skimmia* and spring bulbs

Tour of the Garden

The Rill Garden

The walled garden, with its pools and canalised stream, was originally planted exclusively with roses, which do not thrive in this humid maritime climate. Today the central island beds are now predominately planted with a mixture of hardy herbacious and semi-tender perennials of soft pastel shades to create a relaxed and dreamy effect. In the borders adjacent to the walls is a collection of unusual climbers and shrubs taking advantage of the extra protection offered. They include the twinning climber *Dregea sinensis* from China, the Chilean Mitre Flower, and fragrant Ginger lilies from India with their spidery yellow and orange flowers, and a *Buddleja lindleyana* from Japan. Above the Rill Garden are a fine Westfelton Yew, overhanging the circular steps, and a Cut-leaved Beech of great elegance. On the outside wall are several Callicarpas with their autumnal magenta to purple tinted berries, a *Rhaphiolepis umbellata* and several Cestrums and Abutilons.

The Terraces

Around the house the garden has a firm architectural framework, with walls and terraces which reflect the lines of the house. They are used to shelter tender, mainly sunloving plants including: the Mexican yucca-like *Beschorneria*, a large flowered Butterfly Bush; the banana-scented *Michelia*; a *Camellia sasanqua*, which produces its fragrant deep pink flowers in autumn; *Leptospermums* or New Zealand Tea Trees in crimson and pink; Wandflowers and Watsonias. The house walls shelter a number of fine climbers and wall shrubs, including sweetly perfumed Holboellia, Wintersweet, a red and yellow Abutilon, Crape Myrtle, Chilean Jasmine, and the autumn flowering *Sparmannia africana*. Each terrace has a pool; the upper, concave pool especially echoes the work of Lutyens. Its rounded outline sets off a sculptured otter, by local artist Bridget McCrum, reflected in the otherwise clear water. The lower terrace is divided by a larger, rectangular pool, in which grows the Water Hawthorn, with its fragrant black-anthered, white flowers in spring.

The Stream

As you wander down the garden, past Spring displays of iris and primulas, the dominant tree you pass is a large *Liriodendron tulipifera* resplendent in early summer with its tulip shaped green-yellow and orange flowers. Few trees can have such presence – yet it dates only from 1926. Below it are two interesting deciduous conifers: the Dawn Redwood (discovered in the wild only in 1941) and the Swamp Cypress, with its much finer alternate leaves. Both colour attractively in autumn before the leaves fall, setting off the brilliant scarlet of the Japanese Maples by the stream. The bark of the nearby Chilean Myrtle, smooth and cinnamon-brown, is handsome all year round. Near the lower pond Dianellas, with evergreen iris-like leaves, produce their pale blue flowers followed by long-lasting oblong berries in rich royal blue.

The Lower Terrace border in midsummer with Penstemons, Gazaneas, Cuphea and Salvias

The Rill Garden

(*Opposite*) The constantly running stream keeps the garden moist throughout the year

Bowling Green Lawn and the Gazebo

By taking the middle terrace path past the Chilean Lantern Trees and the Otter Pool you reach the Bowling Green Lawn with Wellington's Wall, a south facing raised bed to your left harbouring sun loving plants such as Cistus, Romneya, Rosemary and Gaura. Ahead lies the path to the Gazebo passing plantings of exotics like yuccas, bromeliads, proteas and echiums. (You can divert at this point and take the Paddock Wood path for a fine view of the sea and the Mewstone, a rocky island to the west). At the Gazebo the lower garden is spread before you like a vast amphitheatre. Below you is the quarry, where the stone for the house was taken; before you a view of the sea and the Blackstone rocks, framed by pines. From the Gazebo the dominant tree is the tall Tree of Heaven to your right.

Cathedral Bank

The path from the Gazebo leads past banks of blue and white African Lilies through a wooded area, where among others a Snowdrop Tree, two Handkerchief Trees and several flowering dogwoods grow. Past the shelter belt the path emerges above a wide slope to reveal another fine sea view.

The Middle and Lower Garden

Turning back, you come to the foot of the quarry, and take the central path for a short distance, between a massive clump of bamboo with canes up to 2.5 cm across and the ferny leaved Mimosa (*Acacia dealbata*). Nearby grows a thicket of the Sweet Pepper Bush with its fragrant white flowers in late summer and a Loquat. You pass beneath a tall evergreen dogwood (*Cornus capitata*), which is laden in spring with creamy-yellow flowers and in the autumn with red, strawberry like fruits. Two rare relatives of the Protea grow closeby, *Gevuina avellana* and *Lomatia ferruginea*, both with striking foliage.

It is possible here to turn right and cross a granite bridge beneath the towering Tree of Heaven (*Ailanthus altissima*) and past a group of Calico bushes. Here, among others, are big scented *loderi* rhododendrons, their peeling trunks handsome all year round. A little further one reaches the Lower Pond with its gigantic rhubarb-like leaves of the Gunnera fringing the waters edge. Beyond the path divides, the left fork taking you back to the Rill Garden passed the largest *Cotoneaster watereri* in the country, and a huge Persian Ironwood Tree.

If you continue down the main path, on both sides are several magnolias, flowering in succession; the latest to flower, a hybrid with creamy-buff flowers, fills this part of the garden with its aromatic perfume in early summer. Here too, on your left, is the black stemmed bamboo *Phyllostachys nigra*. Soon you pass the twin Cypress Oaks standing at the foot of Cathedral Bank before arriving at the lower garden, dell like in character, with its rustic styled chestnut bridge, hydrangeas and New Zealand Tree Ferns underplanted with *Geranium maderense*, a tender geranium from Madeira. Access through a gate leads you onto the coastal footpath and to the viewing point at the head of Pudcombe Cove.

Magnolia × wiesneri

The Gazebo provides superb views over the garden and the sea

(*Opposite*) The steep banks of the garden are covered with wild garlic and other wild flowers in spring

In spring the garden is filled with carpets of bluebells

The Lower Pond is shaded by the large leaves of *Gunnera manicata* from Brazil

Newfoundland

It is worth returning by an alternative path to the left of the stream, beneath a large spreading beech, and past the dramatic rock outcrop known as Newfoundland. Continuing up the steps one reaches a glade in which grows several interesting trees including a *Podocarpus totara* and a *Pittosporum eugenioïdes* '*Variegatum*' from New Zealand, and a *Sciadopitys verticillata* or Japanese Umbrella Pine. By following the narrow path under elegant bamboos and across two small rustic bridges you may regain the main path.

The Valley Slopes

For those with enough energy, continuing up the steps brings you via the Bluebell Wood to the West Banks with its excellent views across the valley garden and offering paths on several levels to explore. Being an area of unimproved grassland, during the spring and summer months it is covered with a profusion of wildflowers and fine grasses attracting an interesting variety of insects and butterflies adding to the wonderful diversity of wildlife in the garden.

You can return to the Visitor Centre via the Rill Garden and the Upper Garden to the main drive passing a fine shrubby North American Horse Chestnut (*Aesculus parviflora*), and in the spring, flowering bulbs and hellebores.

Paths criss-cross the valley slopes

The D'Oyly Cartes bought the estate for this view